BLUE COLLAR POET

101 POEMS

ROCKY RHOADS

authorHOUSE®

AuthorHouse™
1663 Liberty Drive
Bloomington, IN 47403
www.authorhouse.com
Phone: 1 (800) 839-8640

Published by AuthorHouse 10/19/2017

ISBN: 978-1-5462-1146-4 (sc)
ISBN: 978-1-5462-1145-7 (e)

Print information available on the last page.

This book is printed on acid-free paper.

CONTENTS

ME

The Natural World And Its Creatures

Of God And Men

ME

BLUE-COLLAR POET

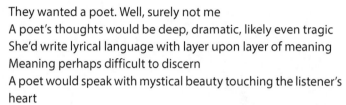

They wanted a poet. Well, surely not me
A poet's thoughts would be deep, dramatic, likely even tragic
She'd write lyrical language with layer upon layer of meaning
Meaning perhaps difficult to discern
A poet would speak with mystical beauty touching the listener's
heart
A poet would delve into the soul to find its hidden emotions
To find its buried fears and illuminate its inner glory
A poet's humor would be lofty, a sophisticated dance with words

None of those are true when I write, I am no sophisticate
The words are simple, only one meaning and it ever so clear
If pathos is there it is plain, humor perhaps a bit earthy
Most emotions presented unvarnished
Yet I have need to write the words that whirl in my head
To see them flow across paper
Perhaps I should introduce myself as,
"Hi, I 'm Rocky, just a blue-collar poet"

RIPE OLD AGE

How wonderful, he said
You've reached a ripe old age
Ripe old age
Now that's a strange phrase for you
What do you think it means?
Age? Yeah, I know about that
Old? Oh yeah, I know more every day
But ripe? Ripe. . .
What picture does that paint?
Perhaps a grape vine heavy with fruit
Purple and bursting with juice
Such a beautiful image
Doesn't match what my mirror shows
More like grapes starting to wrinkle
Even half way to being raisins!
I suppose if you think in opposites
Ripe as opposed to raw and untested
Then it becomes a good thing
Who wants to be seen as callow?
I wouldn't mind being called seasoned
Or experienced or wise
But ripe somehow suggests to me
That just around the corner lies rot
And while rot may lie just around my corner
I'd rather not hear it said out loud.

PARALLEL PARKING

They say never stop learning
Keep finding challenge in your life
Sounds good in theory
Becomes scary in reality
My parking place was gone
The one always there for me
The street was packed
So, what was I gonna do?
Well I drove round the block
Hoping things had changed
Same song, second verse
My parking place
Still ocupado
But just ahead of that
A small empty space
Did I dare?
I can't parallel park
Done it twice in my life
Intimidating doesn't begin to cover it
Calling this a challenge
Is to call Mt. Everest a medium difficulty climb
Flip side of that is
I'm pushing 80
If I'm ever to conquer those challenges
I'd better get with the program
So, I hugged a driveway till no cars approached
Pulled my car into position
And started the parallel park
Just the way the book used to say
By golly that Suzuki slid into that spot
Like a well-oiled bullet into the chamber
My day was made!!! I stood outside my car

Just basking in my pride.
Tried to think what friends would be home
That I could call and brag to
Decided not to tell right away
I could glory in it all by myself.

THE SCENT OF A MAN

Went to the dentist today, hardly a romantic outing
But, as I lay back in the reclined chair with my eyes closed
He leaned in to search out the recesses of my mouth
And I caught the faint whiff of a nice aftershave
Something stirred in me, a memory
Of being in a man's arms
I seldom miss having a man around
Rarely even have it cross my mind
I like being on my own
Over 10 years since I was in a marriage
(Twenty-two years alone before that)
And never lonely during those years
As I often was when married
Still, this scent that remained familiar
Evoked in me the half-buried feeling
Of being held securely, in soft safety,
By a man who loved me and whom I loved
It was a long time ago
But the scent of a man remained.

THE STILL OF THE NIGHT

The still of the night
More still than I had thought
Lonely and silent
The horizon of life
Seeming nearer each breath
The small terrors of my soul
Loom loud in the silence
Heard by none by me
Yet I am used to them
The companions of my years
They echo through the darkness
In the still of the night

TOO SOON

Quilt drawn to her chin
Eyes closed and sunken deep
Gravity having its way
Room cloaked in silence
Death watching from the corners
She wakes, is glad to see us
And she lurks behind that smile
Yet is difficult to pin down
Is she present or not?
Some moments are real
Some laughs the laughs of the past
Some looks are bottomless
With only a void behind them
We are stepping in quicksand
Not knowing what to expect
Our love is deep as ever
Her body is real, though frail
Yet our friend only partially here
And dimming before our eyes
A vision in route to a memory
Far, far too soon

SUPREME MOMENT

Behold the turkey
He heralds each dawn
As he struts in his pride
He stands with the pilgrim
As symbol of our heritage
He holds a position of honor
In American lore
Yet, the turkey is ridiculous
Watch him! His actions are silly
He is witless, arrogant, absurd
Still, he does look superb
Regal, and so commanding
In his supreme moment…
On a platter

Well, then, behold me
I'm proud and I sometimes strut
I'm a symbol of nothing
But I'd like to be
A position of honor sounds great
And, I think, would be richly deserved
There are times when I am witless
My actions silly and absurd
I wonder if I'll look commanding
Or, for that matter,
Where I will be…
In my supreme moment.

WORDS FOR A LOVER

Come into my world
Come gently
So not to bruise
But come not timidly
For you are invited
As guest to honor
As mate to love
As lover to touch
Come softly as the cloud
That silently yields
As it touches the mountain
Then comes together
To surround the mountain
In its downy embrace
Yet parts again
And the mountain is seen
Unmoved and unchanged
May we warm each other
In the constant mist of our love
Yet ever be willing to part that cloud
When the ray of another sun
Is needed to make us complete
Always knowing that we will touch again
Come into my world
Come not timidly
For you are loved

UNTETHERED FEELINGS

Stray feelings
Unattached to any thought
Like threads from a web
Forever seeking a rafter

THESE HANDS

These hands are the hands of a nurse.

These hands have delivered new life when no physician was near and they have placed that new life in the welcoming arms of the woman who labored to bring it forth.

These hands have rocked the infant whose body was afire with pain but who was too young to grasp words of explanation.

These hands have held the child whose mother just died and who then knew only fear.

These hands have soothed the brow of the boy whose fever raged.

These hands have dressed the wounds of the biker whose body would heal but whose brain would not.

These hands have cleaned the blood and the stool from the comatose woman.

These hands have restarted the heart of the father whose children stood stricken beyond the drape.

These hands have wiped the tears from the rheumy eyes of the old woman whose body had betrayed her, whose mind was attempting to leave her and whose children had already done so.

These hands have closed the eyes and washed the body of the old man who finally found release from unrelenting pain.

These hands have held in joy the hands of those whose loved one survived, and held in sorrow the hands of those whose loved one perished.

These hands are the hands of a nurse.

These hands are my hands.

What do they do now?

THE UNSEEN WOUND

Internal bleeding
Doesn't show
But the blood is real
The wound is deep
It may seep slowly
Sapping strength
It may gush
And get it over with
I'd prefer the latter
But feel I am slowly seeping
All the good
That is in me
Out into the soil
Blood red soil

TENDERNESS

The loving touch of a mother's hand
On the downy peach of her baby's cheek
There could be no tenderness greater
And yet . . .

Fires of passion flamed high
Flying mindlessly through the clouds
Flames slowly becoming memory
On the gentle return to earth

The kiss of cloth on my skin
As he washed the sweat from my body
The whispery breath on his lips
As he spoke my name to my mouth
The caressing touch of his hands
As they gently feathered my face
The love seen deep in his eyes
As his gaze closed out the world

That was tenderness
Complete

THE SECOND DANIEL

Pain once lived should cease to be
It should halt its ragged breath
Loose its clawed grip on my being
And die

But pain feeds upon itself
As seasons cycle
So, it crowds back into my awareness
And will not die

Child of my child
Is there no better path?
What can we do?
What have we done?

Son of my son
Our love meant no harm
Still no generation escapes
The legacy of darkness

SNOW GLOBE

Well, the holidays finally came and now they are gone
Time to take down the lights and put away the snow globes
You remember snow globes, of course,
Give them a shake and the snow swirls and swirls
Obscuring everything until finally it clears
That's sort of what it felt like
The bright lights of fun and food and family
Taking place in the topsy-turvy world of a snow globe
One that's been given a good, hard shake
And everything has gone swirling too long
Too much noise, too many people, too much sugar
The cat clearly irritated and causing trouble
Crumpled paper in the living room and mud in the kitchen
Icy streets that kept us home on Christmas Eve
And air too cold to breathe that was seeping into the house
But also, excitement in the eyes of one
Who'd not watched a snowfall before
Or awakened to a sparkly white world
And the family around the table for chili
And the warmth of their laughter together
All of the hectic confusion tempered by love
Life in a swirling snow globe is not too bad after all
Can't wait for next year

THE PAST

I spoke to the past
But heard no reply
Nor whispering echo
From the silent void

The mind remained calm
Heartstrings untwisted
How can this be?
So much of life spent
And nothing remains
Of him

PLUMBING

Next to family, sustenance and shelter
Plumbing should be nearest the heart
For a plumber, that is
Not for me
And yet, it is
My personal plumbing that is
If I fail to keep one tap open and working
Or the other tap from having a drip
Without benefit of turning the handle
My whole existence gets screwed
So, the first thing I think in the morning
And the last thing I think of at night
"Did I drink enough water?"
"Will the Imipramine work?"

THE HOSPITAL

I lie awake in the deep hours of the night
The pain much diminished by the haze of Dilaudid
The room full of small lights and shadows and sound
Hospital rooms never silent nor completely dark
I listen to the sound of my children breathing
My daughter stretched out on the couch
My son lying back in the reclined chair
Each covered with but a thin cotton blanket
In a room that is very chill
A room not built for comfort
And I think they should be home sleeping
Resting before their work days
But memories stir of holding them in my arms
Rocking them through teething and falls and fevers
I remember waking during nights gone suddenly cold
And creeping into their rooms to cover them
Role reversal has such a sterile sound
I would never have believed
That I could find it acceptable
But now, so clearly offered with love
I find it warmly comforting and secure
As if they are rocking me in their arms
I do love them so

SILKEN LADDER

The clouds are lovely
Thin and wispy
In horizontal stripes
Like a silken ladder
Leaning against
A wall of blue
Gone higher than I can see

If I should climb
Those silken threads
What would I see?
Would I see neon stars?
Shiny rings around Saturn?
Would there be rocket ships
And meteors on fire?

Or would I look down
And see earth's blue orb
To find that earth's mystery
Echoes the mystery of heaven?
Or perhaps see a kindly old patriarch
With flowing white beard
Welcoming me to his home?

I wonder when
I shall climb that ladder

LOST SOUND

The sound of his voice
Such power to move me
For good or for bad
I no longer remember
The sound of his voice
Oh, I would know it if I heard it
The dream that cannot happen
There is such sorrow in loss
Even the loss of a sound

LOSING WEIGHT

I wanted to lose weight
It's a grand thing to lose weight
(Unless you don't need to lose that is
And they say there are such people)
But for me it would have been grander
If I could have selected the sites
If I'm doing all the work
I should get to say where
Nothing strange about my requests
You know, the upholstered parts
Where the padding is thick, thicker or thickest
But did it happen that way?
Are you kidding? No way.
First, I lost from my face
Granted, I discovered cheek bones
But paid for them with many new wrinkles
Next, I lost from my thighs
Didn't need to lose from my thighs
(Well, maybe I did need to
But my thighs never show so why?!)
Then came my earlobes and heels
And other inappropriate spots
Still, the icing on this bitter cake
Came when I found I had changed
From a 38D to a 34 long
There's something just wrong about
Having to roll'em up before you stuff'em in
Oh, the process had started well before
Gravity is just such a bully
But this time loss outpaced gravity
Like the tortoise outpaced the hare
Oh, and another thing, all that leftover skin!

It just sort of hangs there
Much like a dollar store curtain
And if I turn to the right, it sways to the left
Folks my age can't donate their organs
But I found out old folks can donate skin
And I thought Aha! A use for it
They were polite in refusing my offer
Seems they want me to be dead first
So, for now I'll just go with the sway
Try to lose a little bit more
And hope for the best.

MAN IN THE PARK

The afternoon was hot and muggy
We'd spent a long while at the monuments
My husband had not been to D.C. before
The memorials moved him deeply
As they did me each time I saw them
But we were tired and very hot
He suggested we get ice cream
And sit in the shade for a while
I chose a frozen Dove Bar
Feeling decadent in the choosing
We found a shady bench and sat
The Dove Bar was cool on my tongue
It tasted so good but it was too much
And I couldn't finish it
Threw the rest away in the
Barrel behind our bench
Wasteful

He was tall and dark skinned
Wearing a tattered military jacket
His hair an unkempt afro
I hadn't seen him coming
But before I was fully seated
He was at the barrel behind us
Picking out the rest of the Dove Bar
He walked off down the grass
Eating the bar as he went
My guilt at being wasteful
Remained deep but overshadowed
By shame at my life's abundance
And my failure to remember this
But also, a surprising degree of joy

That if he had to live that way
Or even chose to do so
What I chose to discard
Became food for him
It became cool on his tongue
On that hot, muggy afternoon
Wasteful but not wasted

I WISH I COULD REMEMBER

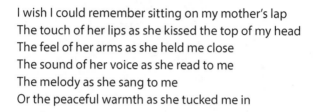

I wish I could remember sitting on my mother's lap
The touch of her lips as she kissed the top of my head
The feel of her arms as she held me close
The sound of her voice as she read to me
The melody as she sang to me
Or the peaceful warmth as she tucked me in

Those are not memories that I have
Did she do any of those things?
Perhaps before I was two she might have
And I simply cannot recall
But the world changed when I became two
My aunt moved in with us

Mimi took over my life
Did she read to me? Word by word she did
As she sounded each out to teach me
Flash cards more than books
She was a teacher
And I had become a student

This aunt did not hold me
Or kiss the top of my head
I never sat on her lap
But she became the tooth fairy
And if she was gone
The fairy was gone also

Mother moved into the back seat
Willingly? There is no way for me to know
Did it cause her great pain?
How could it not? Her child now gone

Into the care of another
Her husband openly adored by the other

The years brought great shame
As I grew old enough to see
The truth for what it was
What must have been bitter for mother
Was stale with guilt for me
There was no room for hugs

I wish I could remember
I cannot remember what did not happen.

HONORED BY GRIEF?

I forgot
There is no other way to say it
I simply forgot
Two days a year I had never forgotten
The day he was born
A day to celebrate
And the day that he died
A day of sorrow and silent grief
Not shared, just felt
This year I didn't honor the day of his death
It just never occurred to me
Six days later when I realized
The realization cascaded into guilt
Heart breaking, gut wrenching guilt
How could I not have remembered?
Why hadn't I honored his memory?
Did it mean that caring had ceased?
No, I knew that was not so
Still I asked it over and over
Then the thought crept in
And has dwelt there ever since
Perhaps he would not feel honored by grief

LAPPED

OK, so I was lapped
The cheery faces I saw as I began
Walking round the lake
I saw again. Twins, perhaps?
Um, probably not
Embarrassing? Well, yeah,
But not exactly a big deal
After all I'm a creaky old broad
Pushing a four-wheeled walker
But, when some of them lapped me again
I began averting my eyes
After all, there's the lake to see
With sunlight dancing in pin points
Over the dark, iris blue water
Well worth the looking
But then! Please say it isn't so
Have I seen this one three times before?
Couldn't be. Could Not Be So!
Oh, it's so, alright
Once, twice, thrice
I've been lapped a third time
By this skinny young thing with a pedometer on
And calves that knot with each step
And, she is jogging, no less!
That haughty look on her face
Could be just a squint from the sun
Or, perhaps she really is thinking
What it looks like she is thinking
But, little does she know
Fifty, sixty years will go in a flash
And she could become me
Grateful just to be walking

Glad for mechanical aids
That help the snail win the race
That's when she'll come to know
That sunlight dancing in pin points
Over the dark, iris blue water
Is better seen at my pace than hers

HOPE DIES AT THE CARWASH

Inside my head and body
Everything lies crumpled
Not dead, just crumpled
As though
When hope fades
Substance follows
As though the enormity
Of unsolvable problems
Puts all systems on shut down
Ah, God, I want so to help
But nothing I do has impact
With that knowledge, hope dies

I HAVE A DREAM

I have a dream
Not, sadly, like Martin Luther King's
MLK's was to benefit mankind
Mine, fulfilled, would benefit me
I'd like to sleep soundly
Through a long, dreamy night
And wake up six inches taller
Or four inches
Or even two

I'd like to see what a top shelf looks like
Or even a middle shelf
I'd like to see over the six-year-old
Seated in front of me
And watch, instead of just hear,
The performers on the stage
I'd like to look, without using a stool
Out the peep hole in the front door

I'm sorry to sound ungrateful
It's a privilege to see at all
And there are many who can't
Still, like Tevye wanting to be rich
It doesn't seem a lot to ask
Just six inches taller
Or four inches
Or two

FILMY BLACK SCARF

A filmy black scarf
Thrown carelessly across the sky
Moving in sinuous rhythm
Through early morning mist
Till between breaths
It is gone

In its place a flock of ravens
Answering some ancient call
Their silhouettes hazy
Their war cries muted
Through the heavy air

The same call stirs in me
Let me take wing and join them
Searching for answers
Searching for battle

Yet my wings stay still
For I am rooted in the soil
And the soil grows no answers
Only battles that cannot be won

Still, the yearning is real
If I could tear loose these roots
If I could but take flight
I would become
A filmy black scarf
I would, oh I would

EVERYDAY GIFTS

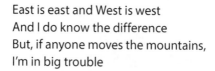

East is east and West is west
And I do know the difference
But, if anyone moves the mountains,
I'm in big trouble

So, I'm thankful for the everyday things,
Like God putting the mountains on the west
And then not moving them
And making them big enough to see
And giving me dogs that don't bark
And a house with no mice
And a roof with no leaks
Family who don't try to change me
And friends who don't tattle
And the freedom from worry
About protecting a fortune
And the tendency to see
Most people and events
As lovely, or humorous
And the strength to deal with them
When they are neither

Extraordinary blessings are beautiful
To be enjoyed to the max
But life mostly consists
Of everyday gifts in such number
That we take them for granted
And when we do that
We don't lose the gifts
We just miss the joy

THE FRIEND

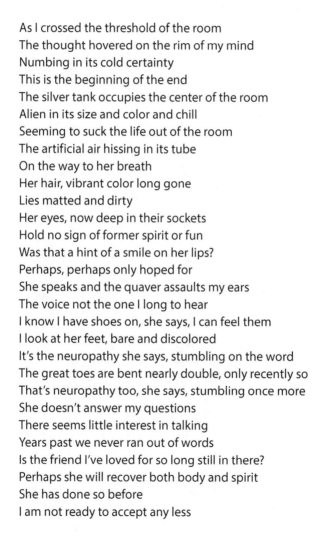

As I crossed the threshold of the room
The thought hovered on the rim of my mind
Numbing in its cold certainty
This is the beginning of the end
The silver tank occupies the center of the room
Alien in its size and color and chill
Seeming to suck the life out of the room
The artificial air hissing in its tube
On the way to her breath
Her hair, vibrant color long gone
Lies matted and dirty
Her eyes, now deep in their sockets
Hold no sign of former spirit or fun
Was that a hint of a smile on her lips?
Perhaps, perhaps only hoped for
She speaks and the quaver assaults my ears
The voice not the one I long to hear
I know I have shoes on, she says, I can feel them
I look at her feet, bare and discolored
It's the neuropathy she says, stumbling on the word
The great toes are bent nearly double, only recently so
That's neuropathy too, she says, stumbling once more
She doesn't answer my questions
There seems little interest in talking
Years past we never ran out of words
Is the friend I've loved for so long still in there?
Perhaps she will recover both body and spirit
She has done so before
I am not ready to accept any less

POST SCRIPT

Neither life nor death wait for "Ready"
Death came last night
And left a deep void behind

FAMILY BONDS

We are bound tightly together
By multiple ribbons silken soft
The feel is not of restriction
But, rather, security and strength
The safety of loving and being loved
The wispy strands of ribbon
Have strength of corded steel
To keep us protected
Within the cocoon of family
Yet one ephemeral ribbon
Can shatter as a sheet of ice
Under footfalls of carelessness
Pain can invade the cocoon
And bruise the hearts of all
Still, love is encoded in our genes
Cells linked by the mystery of ages
Even when one ribbon is torn
The gossamer strands of others
Stay strong and pliant
To bind us and hold us safe
Yet bend as our movements need
Hurt and pain will recede
The warmth of love will endure.

EMPTINESS

Thoughts roam in my head
Stray thoughts escape
To echo off the walls
Of the silent room
Am I lonely?
No, but I am aware
Of the presence now gone
Of the emptiness

HAVING FUN

Do you jog every day
In the sun or the rain?
Do you drink wheat germ malts
And devour yogurt plain?

Do you forego caffeine
And read books on nutrition?
Do you sleep eight hours soundly
To protect your condition?

Do you carefully check
Daily market quotations
And change your investments
To counter inflation?

If you want my opinion
Well, I'll give you a cheer!
You'll be healthy and wealthy
And more so each year.

While I'll keep drinking coffee,
I'll eat pizza with cheese,
I'll buy nitrated bacon
And have wine when I please.

I'll squander my money
On books bad for the mind,
Stay up late at night
At each party I find.

And when the dust settles,
When all's said and done,
We'll just talk it over
To see who had the most fun.

DOVE MEMORY

There on the dew-covered grass
Early that morning
I heard the sound of the dove
A tremulous coo from far away
A murmur so soft yet so clear
Suddenly I was back
In the days of my childhood
When summer mornings
Were always spent
Wrapped in the shade of a tree
Listening to the dove's sweet voice
Loveliest part of the day
Loveliest part of my memories

COLORS

I smiled at her in the parking lot
She smiled back
"I like your white hair," she said
"Reminds me of my friend Mary Alice"
Never thought of my hair as white
More silver gray I thought

But, cut and examined
There is white and silver
Gray and darker
A very few almost black
A mixture just like the rest of me

Oh, I am truly a mixture
Some good, some wicked
Some healthy, some damaged
Some giving, some greedy
Some resilient, some fragile
Some funny, some sad
Some so rigid and needy

The mixture in my hair
As the mixture in me
Doesn't really show
When you look at me
No one really knows
All the colors in my hair
Or all the colors that are me

WINTER WINDOW

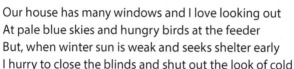

Our house has many windows and I love looking out
At pale blue skies and hungry birds at the feeder
But, when winter sun is weak and seeks shelter early
I hurry to close the blinds and shut out the look of cold
Except for the window in my room

There, across the midnight grounds, a light atop a high pole
Casts a glimmering pool on the snow, with only shadows
Of bare black trees to break the dim white carpet of snow
Silence is profound though only seen, not heard

A night scene, perhaps, from an old film
Bogart might stroll through, trench coat belted
Collar up, fedora turned down,
To slip soundlessly into darkness that rims the light

Such a scene might make me fearful
Yet it holds no terror for me
The shadows and light are lovely
The stillness speaks of peace

They say if you stand alone on the shore
When your heart is full of despair
Sirens of the sea will beckon to you
And fear will be gone with the first soft step
Into the promised rest

Perhaps my window scene holds sirens of the night
For it calls out to me, it beckons
And that small sliver of despair
That dwells in the back of my soul wants to respond
To find that promised rest

COMPUTERS

Don't know how computers work
Or how they were ever invented
Know fabulous things are done on computers
Folks use them to write documents
To communicate with friends and colleagues
To record their finances and do graphic art
We'd be in a mess without them
But from my very own perspective
While I love to get emails
And I'd hate to go all the way back
To using my IBM Selectric
To accomplish all of my writing
My lap top seems to have one main function
To cause me frustration, pure and simple
I find myself stymied again and again
What is simple for my daughter
Defeats me at turn after turn
What is logical to my son
Makes no sense at all to me
I try very hard to do it just right
But something always seems to go wrong
Then my blood pressure spikes
And my confidence tanks
And I wonder if my local Goodwill store
Has any Selectrics in stock

CHEMICAL TEARS

Tears of grief are different
Containing chemicals
Not found in other tears
So, I have read
Chemicals meant to cleanse?
To scrub the toxins of sorrow?
Years have come and gone
Are tears today the same?
Or have chemicals evaporated
Leaving tears to shed
With no special significance
On the face that is seen
Or in the dark canyons of the soul
Do tears flow yet
Bitter with the chemicals
That never cleanse

AGELESS

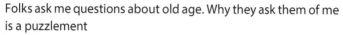

Folks ask me questions about old age. Why they ask them of me
is a puzzlement
But, not wanting to seem impolite, I try to come up with the
answers
How have you changed, they ask, as you age?
Well, my skin has new wrinkles and folds, as well as bumps, tags,
warts and moles
My joints now are filled with Rice Krispies, you can tell from their
snap, crackle, pop
And insomnia? The Innocent sleep no more

What losses, they ask, occur as you age?
Well, sphincter control leaps to mind
And there was the ability to get myself up once I had got myself
down
You've heard "My get up and go has got up and went."
Mine got up and went alright, taking my memory with it
Used to remember what books I had read
Used to be able to call you by name
But those data banks can no longer be accessed

Surely, you've made gains on the way they ask, have you gained
knowledge?
Oh, I reply, that is the expectation but I don't think I've gained
knowledge
Or if I did I've forgotten what it was
Have you gained patience they ask?
Well you know, there's a problem with that, I'm sure I've gained
plenty of patience
But I get so darned irritated I can't take time to look for it

Perhaps the most disconcerting change is listening when the youngsters talk
Youngster being defined as anyone less than 65
There is such a disconnect with language, I hear them and wonder, is that Swahili?
They talk only in high tech terms that have no meaning for me
Do you remember the Wendy's ad, 'Where's the beef'?"
If so, you must be old too
I use phrases like that, they seem everyday stuff to me
The youngsters look at me as if I'm the one speaking Swahili

The subject of jury duty came up
They allow us "over the hillers" to opt out of jury duty
I said that was a shame, We're the ones with lots of free time
My daughter quietly mentioned, Mom
There are no porta-potties in the court room
Good point! Said I

CHOCOLATE

Ah, Valentine's Day, how romantic!
Full of tender emotions for me
A time made to share with my lover
Or eat chocolate if all lovers flee
Well, a girl has to look to her future
Make plans for days stormy or fair
Cause men seem to come and go quickly
But chocolate will always be there

Oh, beware of those soul stirring glances
Of the words that fall soft on the ear
Don't buy all those tender sweet nothings
They can never be trusted my dear
So, to help you prevent tears and heartache
These words of pure wisdom I share
That men are just naturally fickle
But, chocolate will always be there

BEING CENTER

Difficult dance
Fraught with pain
And laced with fear
Being center
Between loves

COLD AND COLDER

I'm old, and gettin' older
I'm cold, and gettin' colder
She's younger, cold she's not
She's active and she gets hot

She's in her shorts, her arms are bare
I'm in my woolen underwear
She doesn't like to see me freeze
She'll turn the heat up just to please

I don't know how she stays so warm
When chilblains seem to be my norm
I shiver, pack more layers on
Till mobility's completely gone

Over the long johns a turtleneck tight
Sweat shirt and sweater, buttoned just right
Leg warmers feel so snug and so soft
And fur lined slippers cap it all off

Hand warmers work for the end of the fingers
For the rest of the hand the cold still lingers
The answer to that is the half finger mitten
And that, my dear friends, is all I have written

ANXIETY

Anxiety is:
A four-letter word plus three
With no value to me,
Or to those in my life
A huge waste of emotion,
Of time and energy
Corrosive to relationships
And to self-satisfaction
A source of fear and pain
Ridiculous and absurd
A brain immobilizer
Free but still costly
With penalties so obvious
A dunce would know to avoid
Yet my greatest pitfall
Totally self-induced
My near constant companion
Anxiety is: Me

ANOTHER DAY?

I walk among the trees
The branches of each entwine with another
Allowing little light to guide my feet
Little warmth to melt my chill
Bottom branches hang heavy and low
I cannot tell what is substance
And what is merely shadow
I yearn for light and warmth
But find them not
My heart lies crumpled within me
Crying to soar in open space
But my wings stay tightly folded
Open skies remain invisible
Even the pathway now hidden
Doorway closed and locked
My wings must stay folded
I cannot soar
Another day perhaps?

LOVER

I am not alone this evening
There's a companion by my side
Not the lover of choice
His name is fatigue
No romantic is he
Not gentle, nor sweet
But faithful? Ah, yes
He cannot be tempted
Away from my side
Still, if fortune smiles
He will caress me to sleep
Yet be gone in the morning
His touch tonight
Not requiring
That I fix breakfast

HOW CAN IT BE?

How can it be
That the age I feel
Is not the age you see
That what I once thought was old
Is now my everyday norm
That the stoop I'd have pitied
I now wear as a coat

How can it be
That hands once so strong
Can no longer open the jar
Fingers once so nimble
Can no longer grasp the pill
Or bring it safely to my lips
Only to be so hard to swallow

How can it be
That I need things such as pills
That my blood runs so cold
That my steps, though still strong
Can leave pain in their wake
And my hair, once so thick
Now thins and goes white

How can it be
That the years have marched by
Without taking the child within me
The child I still feel
Who still wants to play
And get ready for life
How can it be?

THE NATURAL WORLD
AND ITS CREATURES

TULIP TALK

The old house is dull red brick
Dingy grey wall in front
Trees still winter dead
Grass withered brown
But, amidst that brown I see
Dark green shafts newly grown
And standing tall among them
Straight, slender, imperious
Are living claret cups
Raucous red and yowling yellow
The brilliant blossoms
Proclaim so proudly,
And right in your face,
"We are tulips
We bow to no one
We are first to live
Deserving first breath
To outshine all
We are tulips"
Arrogant beauty

THE WIND

I do not like wind, it weakens me
Brings discord to my thoughts
Frailty to my mood
Tonight it is a mournful howl
Joined by the noise of wind thrashed trees
Yet, even though my ears rebel at the assault
I glance through the high window
And there is the round, silver moon
Dimmed only by wisps of grey clouds
Drifting like tendrils of Spanish moss
Across the moon's satiny face
And I see those wind driven trees
Clad in winter's bare coat
The branches I'd thought of as thrashing
Now appear to be dancing
Across that ethereal light
Dancing in mysterious beauty
The scene mesmerizingly lovely
And the noise of the wind disappears

THE SUNFLOWER DID NOT KNOW

What should I call that sky? heavy?
Yes, heavy, leaden sky
Pressing down on the world
Robbing the day of its joy

The sunflower stands against the fence
Straight and tall on its slender stalk
Petals of blazing yellow pouring out
Its own brand of sunshine

The day itself was dingy
Dead beneath that somber sky
But, the sunflower, not knowing,
Went on spilling sunshine

THE STORM

The vivid flash
Of a fiery sky
The scent of rain
On the night air
The shimmering drops
On each tender blade
The mist in my face
The storm has ended
I am in love

THE PANCAKED BUNNY

His tension palpable
Yet perfectly still
Eyes unblinking
No twitch of muscle or hair
Legs splayed out
Belly pressed hard to the earth
Ears laid flat on his skull
He hides deep in the grass
The newly mown lawn
Offering scant protection
From the invading dogs
Still the pancaked bunny
With discipline tight
Eludes the canine hoard
He lives to jump and spin
And pancake another day

WIND WHIPPED CLOUDS

I love seeing the marvels of this world
Nature a vision of glory and life
My first love in all this great bounty
Forever turns out to be clouds
I think of them as snowy white
Fluffy bowls of whipped cream
And often they are
But then, before my eyes
Appears flaming red or deepest black
And every hue in between
No shape exists they have not found
And never the same again
They may be light and ephemeral
Or threatening and heavy
And I marvel at each design they make
Still, ones that steal my heart and mind
Are those whipped high by the winds
Light and lacy, with no apparent substance
As though a brush is dipped in white paint
Then, just a flick of God's wrist
And curlicues and tendrils appear
Feathers and fingers of froth
Foamy whitecaps on a sea of blue
Or streamers carving great arcs
Across the azure dome
It matters not which form I see
Always I'm lost in the dream
Fascinated by the wonder of them
Waiting for what appears next

THE LAKE

I watch the serene waters
Across the lake the mountains
Soft and voluptuous
Green, dark gray, spotted with gold
Where sunlight strikes hill
The giants
Those that reach for the clouds
Are behind, but not seen
From this place
The low, rolling mountains
Are repeated in the water
Perfectly replicated
Though turned on end
A band of green trees divides
One from the other
Beauty seen once again
Ducks and geese float gently
Now and again one flies
Disturbing the water on take off
The water then rippling
Distorts the mountains image
And the picture shimmers
Before returning to itself
A band of geese on the shore
One standing as a heron
On one leg, perfectly balanced
But the webbed foot hanging behind
Disrupts the picture of grace
He turns and walks to the water
The limping gait hard to watch
Balance had come from pain

THE DAY'S CYCLE

Sun rises with rooster's crow
Moon appears at coyote's howl
Earth has fulfilled her long day
And we who love light can rest
Creatures of the dark awaken
To move without sound
Across the land
Through shadows cast by moon
Silence is safety
Stealth is survival
They hunt their prey
Escape their hunters
Guard their young
Search for love
Without sun to give warmth
Or light their way
Through their universe
Parallel to our own
A lifetime outside our hearing
Leaving our slumber undisturbed
Till rooster prepares to crow

SUNRISE

Sunrise, exquisite beauty
Colors vibrant as flames
Blazing across pale sky
I stood in awe and watched
With such a feeling of wonder
The thought crossed my mind
A day that begins with magnificence
Cannot be all bad
So easy as hours pass by
To sink in the mire of defeat
Awe and wonder become lost
As though the sun had not risen
Yet the light of the sun remains
Warming me all the long day
May that warmth carry memory
Of the morning's majesty
May that memory
Keep me afloat
To see the sun rise again

SPRINGTIME IN THE ROCKIES

The cat he is yowling
The wind it is howling
Tree limbs are breaking
The house it is shaking
She planted our flower seed
And the veggies we'd need
Those plants were just born
Then got snowed on this morn
The sky is all gray
No sun the whole day
I'd like to stay cheerful
But I'm damn near tearful
Can't wait for summer
This cold is a bummer

If I gripe in July
Please remind me just why
I begged for some heat
When the cold had me beat
And when the sweat pours off of my brow
Remind me to be
Content with what's now

PEPPER

She jumps into my lap
A lovely creature
Black fur shot through with molten gold
Eyes the shade of ancient amber
Tail a wide swath of smoky chiffon
With golden bands washed pale by the smoke
She settles into a crescent
Presenting herself to be loved
The rhythm of her purr begins
And in mere moments she sleeps
Impossibly soft, impossibly sweet
Suddenly her head snaps to attention
Ears at sharp salute
Responding to some far distant alarm
Completely beyond my ken
And in a blur of motion
She is gone
Leaving behind an empty lap
And the echo of a purr

SNOWY MOUNTAINS

Tallest peaks stand deep in snow
And from a distance
Shimmer as the whitest satin
Lower peaks seem navy blue
Shading into black
Where canyons divide
And before that darkness

Darker yet
A covey of jet black birds
Flying together
In graceful ovals
Dark upon dark
Then rising as a cloud of smoke
The darkest of clouds
Appears on the light blue sky
Darting and wheeling
In loops and arcs
Before winging north

Over the distant horizon
The mountains stand
The birds now a dream

POOLS OF AQUAMARINE

Water, cleft by the prow
Writes delicate script of foam
Silent and silky gauze
Glides past the side of the ship
Feathery as Irish lace
Soft veil of first communion
Dances round glassy pools
Of Aquamarine

Sunlit, diamonds sparkle
Moonlit, emeralds gleam
Slowly, as it passes
Frothy lace fans wider
Larger and larger the pools
Of aquamarine

Now floating gently behind us
Lacy foam moves out and out
Becoming thin as a dream
Then fades into dark satin sea
The pools now indistinct mirrors
Of aquamarine

ODE TO THE EGG

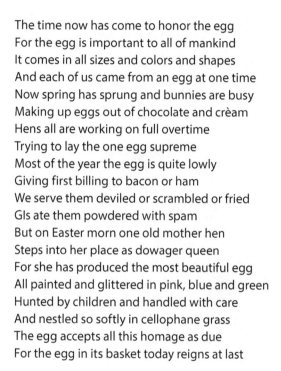

The time now has come to honor the egg
For the egg is important to all of mankind
It comes in all sizes and colors and shapes
And each of us came from an egg at one time
Now spring has sprung and bunnies are busy
Making up eggs out of chocolate and crèam
Hens all are working on full overtime
Trying to lay the one egg supreme
Most of the year the egg is quite lowly
Giving first billing to bacon or ham
We serve them deviled or scrambled or fried
GIs ate them powdered with spam
But on Easter morn one old mother hen
Steps into her place as dowager queen
For she has produced the most beautiful egg
All painted and glittered in pink, blue and green
Hunted by children and handled with care
And nestled so softly in cellophane grass
The egg accepts all this homage as due
For the egg in its basket today reigns at last

RAZZ

Orbs of fiery yellow
Saint to sinner
Sans blink
Caressing touch
Soft as morning mist
Playful wraith
A downy whirlwind
Dark gray smoke
In silent motion
Leaves no trace
Only the memory
Of a purr

LONELY LLAMA

I peer through the fence's wee opening
And view a small slice of green
Where a tiny herd of white goats
Grazes on the short green grass
One wooly brown llama
Stands proudly on guard
He looks so very lonely
Having nothing at all in common
With the herd of dirty white goats
I've watched him there for some years
Standing proud but alone
Today, a second brown llama!
One standing, one lying down
Now pride but no loneliness
My heart is lifted

LIFE AT SNOWMASS

There are ants and bees
And ladybugs and flies
And countless creatures
That crawl or fly
But have no name
I am a minority of one
There are buzzes and drones
And whispers and whirs
In a place of silence
Filled with sounds
Busy sounds of life
That do not disturb the peace
That do not destroy the silence

HAWK AND BIRD

Seated at my breakfast table
A hawk winged past the bay window
Beautiful rust and black colors
Flashing in the sunlight
Marvelous to watch
I followed to another window
Watching him fly onto a tree branch
Then, with a quick duck of his head
He plucked a small bird from that branch
And so, nature provides
Though difficult to watch
The hawk glided to our retaining wall
The bird fluttering in his beak
I couldn't watch him eat that bird
Yet before I could turn away
The hawk flung the bird into the air
The tiny bird began to work his wings
But before he could soar
The hawk flew up and caught him again
I'd seen the videos
Of Orcas playing with baby seals
I'd watched my cat play with a living mouse
But I'd never seen a predator bird
Play with prey he had caught
And it was painful to watch
The hawk threw the bird into the air
Then flew up and caught it
Time after time till it could no longer fly
And fell, stunned, to the ground
Then the hawk jumped to the ground
And prodded the inert bird
With his beak and his talons

He did this many times
But the bird could no longer respond
His life force was gone
The hawk stood for a while
As if confused
Then, finally, consumed the bird
As nature intended
The feast was easier to watch
Than the play had been

FOUR LEGGED LONELINESS

He has stood for many hours
Alone in his field
Patiently waiting and watching
The others of his kind
Separated from him by a fence
A roadway and yet another fence
They, in groups of two or three
Graze in quiet companionship
He has not bent once to the grass
His need for food surely there
But less than his need for the others
He only stands and stares
After many hours
He turns and steps back
Neck arching down he touches grass
Not satisfied he starts to walk
Slowly follows the fence
As if searching a way out
Was he culled for a reason?
Or left behind by chance?
He neither knows nor cares
He knows only the ache of longing
For the presence of others

FEED ME

He hops from branch to branch
Even takes flight if need be
One way or another
He stays by his mother
She busily pecks for insects or seeds
He stands, wings down swept
But fluttering hard
Tiny beak open
Demanding
Feed me, feed me

True, he is larger than she is
And quite capable of feeding himself
But she has always fed him
If he flutters hard enough
And calls loudly enough
Surely she will feed him

And she does

GIZA

Could you please be young again
To match your years to mine?
Could you run and climb the fence
Eat the turkey one more time
Could you take the squirrel's bait
And tear across the lawn
Could you hear the bird's alert
Even before the dawn
Could you be all shiny black
Without one touch of grey,
Could you be that young again
To race through every day
Why did God let you grow old
So far ahead of me?
The loss I know is coming soon
And that day you'll be free
But oh, how I shall mourn for you
When you have gone away
Could you please be young again
Even for just one day?

FULL CYCLE

Leaves fall, driven before the wind
Their legacy is seen, limbs left naked
Without grace or softening color
Standing stark and exposed under leaden skies
That shed no warmth
The death end of the cycle
Yet the barren limbs wait patiently on
For they know that a cycle repeats
Rebirth will come, warmth will return
Limbs no longer naked
Will hang heavy with new leaves
They can depend on the joy of spring

When we fall,
Battered by winds of sorrow and pain
When our very souls stand shamed and exposed
And the whole world can see
That our grace and softness are gone
When we are in
The death end of the cycle
Do we yield to eternal winter
Mired in the cold of our beaten souls
Refusing even to hope for new warmth
Or do we stand waiting with unbowed limbs
Renewing our courage
Knowing that our spring, too
Will come

FIRST FLIGHT

The concrete monolith rising to the sky
Had lines of power carrying light and warmth
On a ledge that circled near the top
Gleaming ravens raised their brood
From my window I saw tiny heads bobbing in the nest
One parent then the other came winging in with food
One day the chicks climbed out of the nest
Four tiny ravens skittering on that ledge
Peering down at the world below
Now the parents circled round and round urging, calling
Showing these new ones how easily they could soar
Years past these parents had fledged each chick with success
Now, finally, one chick took wing,
Flew a few feet, then turned back
But, as his parents pled, he tried again and stayed aloft
Soon another and still another followed
The family winged through the air together
All but the one left on the ledge
Unsteadily, he rounded the ledge time after time
He peered over the edge, he watched the others fly
His yearning was palpable even from so far
The parents brought him food and continued to call
Continued to urge him to follow them
Beneath their harsh caws could be heard the words
"Come on, Baby, you can do it"
But he could not
Over the days the cries of the parents
And their visits with food grew less frequent
Then came the moment I had so dreaded
When through my window I saw the empty ledge
I tried to envision my tiny raven
Gliding the winds with his family

But my aching heart knew it wasn't so
I walked to the base of the monolith
My eyes not wanting to see
There he lay, crumpled and tiny
He had taken his first flight

DEAD AMONG THE LIVING

At Grand Lake we see
Velvet green trees reflected in the lake's still waters
Serene and elegant
But look closely
See the circles of grey midst all the green?
That is death
The towering pines, miracles of growth and strength
Defeated by a tiny insect
Here, death stands among the living.

Where death is not yet vast
The grey looks soft and lovely against the green
As pale green aspen clumps
Contrast with forest around them
So, the misty grey enhances dark green
Then a single tree is seen outlined in blue sky
Its bare limbs have a lacey appearance
Bringing to mind the Spanish moss of a different clime
Again, soft and lovely

Yet travel on as the insect has done
To the land where he has won the battle
Here nothing soft, nothing lovely
Here death is felt and seen, perhaps even heard
Devastation is complete
Where one living green tree still stands
It serves only as a reminder of what was
Of a forest family once vibrant
Now sacrificed to this lowly insect
Man, and his environment, brought low in its wake
To mourn and remember.

CHIPMUNKS

So many chipmunks seen playing in the grass
Some cross the porch at my feet
I place part of a cracker there, "just in case"
Later, as I read, I see a peripheral shadow
Scurry round the corner and then
Two small beady eyes in a brown, furry face
Peer over the edge of the porch
In one upward bound he is there
Lovely striped back and full tail
Maybe 30 inches from my toes
He turns broadside to me and lies down
Belly flat against the stone, eyes staring straight ahead
Yet, every few seconds he whips his head around
Glances at me as I sit motionless
Then stares back straight ahead
Time seems to stand still, till he stands
Turns and picks up the cracker
"Well, now you'll be off" I think, "Hope you enjoy."
But, no, he sits up on his haunches and,
Cracker held between tiny paws, takes a nibble
He eats that cracker down to the very last crumb
Staring straight at me the whole time
Is he showing gratitude? Or daring me to run him off?
Don't know. But I do know he enjoyed it!
And so did I!

DAWN

Dawn creeps in
With feathered breath
Promising warmth
It brushes my cells
And wakens my blood
Still I resist emergence
Not desiring
The harsh light of day
For dreams were reality
And downy soft
Shadowed sleep was not
A dark and fearful place
It was my peaceful haven
And it awaits

COYOTE

His coat was sleek
With lovely colors
A handsome beast
Not scruffy as most
The vision would please
Were it not
For the soft black pelt
He held in his mouth
He also needs food
And nature provides
But gives pain in the doing

CAT IN THE BATH

So, we have this cat named Rasputin, or Razz for short
Or you dumb, damn cat, whatever fits the moment
He is big and feisty and fun, most of the time
Well, he is big all of the time
I decided to take a relaxing hot bath and read
One of life's great pleasures in my mind
I went to fill the tub but found that Razz was in it
Sprawled out across the bottom
He is heavy and hard to pick up anytime
From the bottom of the tub was a real pain
Especially since he didn't wish to depart the tub
But, I finally got him out and got me in
The water was hot and deep and relaxing
The candle was lit and my book was open
Aaaaahhhhhhhhhh
Then the cat appeared and hung over the edge of the tub
He batted the water with his paw and spattered my book
I said, "Please go away nice kitty." Did he go?
Of course not, rather, he jumped onto the edge of the tub
And promptly fell into the water
He discovered, as did I, that digging in with his claws didn't help
To escape the water at all
Until those claws found the flesh of my belly
Then he discovered, as did I, that he could move very fast
If he really dug in deep
Though sopping wet he jumped and flew like greased lightning
I thought, "Good, let him go sulk" until I remembered
He would head for the sunny spot on my quilt
I would have a sopping wet bed!
Now, I am neither fast nor graceful when getting up
Certainly not from the bottom of a tub
And my book fell into the water as I got up

And you could in no way compare me to lightning
Greased or not
But, for me, I was supersonic as I went after that cat
Caught him and toweled him off which he resented immensely
Seemed to think the whole episode was my fault
By then the water was tepid, the book was soaked
And I was out of the mood

AUTUMN

"Fall is my favorite time of year
I love autumn most of all"
A claim I hear from so many
Crisp air, vibrant colors
Descriptors often used
Yet for me this may be artifice
For autumn has cruel intent
Crisp will turn to bitter cold
Vibrant become an empty brown
Memories of fall's beauty gone
Crowded out by reality
Of losses, old and new
Winter will come
Bringing its rawness and cold
Autumn will have fled once more
And left in its place
The bitterness of death

BENEATH THE SEA

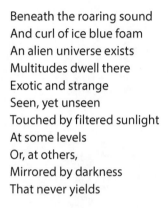

Beneath the roaring sound
And curl of ice blue foam
An alien universe exists
Multitudes dwell there
Exotic and strange
Seen, yet unseen
Touched by filtered sunlight
At some levels
Or, at others,
Mirrored by darkness
That never yields

This unknown life calls me
Yet frightens my very soul
Mystery must remain
For I cannot penetrate
The fertile womb
Of this watery world
The mystery remains

CASANOVA THE CAT

The gentleman cat, Rasputin, resides with us
We call him Razz when we are pleased with him
We call him other things when we are not
He is most handsome with coat of silky smoke
And down of silver white beneath the smoke
The lady cat, Beauty, resides next door
Her coat is shiny black and sleek
Razz finds her lovely indeed
She comes to our glass door to visit
And Razz races to join her
He pirouettes and preens to impress
Bringing to mind a teenaged boy
The Lady Beauty, beyond the glass
Stares intently with bright yellow orbs
Yet shows no sign of response
Razz tries hard to climb through the glass
Determined to reach his lady love
The glass defeats with rigid rebuff
His pleading cries become piteous
We cannot deny such adoration
We take him out to be with the lady
They each hunker down mere inches apart
They stay immobile, carved of stone
Razz utters a low, questioning rumble
Beauty stretches a paw and swats his face, hard
Stunned, Razz jerks back and stares
Then turns tail and flees for his life
His dreams of true love left behind
His golden moment shattered to shards
Casanova the Cat has become Puss the Wuss

OF GOD AND MEN

CRY FOR HER

Cry for her
For she is too tired to live
Yet too frightened to die
Existing only in the space between
Where breath is hard fought
Yet will not cease
And laughter but a memory
Time will bring change
Death's call become stronger
Breath's drive be defeated
Her fear will be drowned
In the turbulent river of fate
As it carries her to warm waters
From whence she came
And from whence she can sail
For quiet beyond the horizon

THE HALOED CRONE

Perhaps she was not a crone
But only looked that way
Bent and wrinkled
With stiff gray hair
Sticking at odd angles

And wearing a halo
Crusted with sequins
And sparkly stars on wires
That fluttered as she walked
Stars a child might wear
With a princess dress

He was tall and thin
With papery arms
And corded neck
He gazed lovingly at her
As she flitted around
In sneakers and silver halo

Alzheimer's?
I wonder
Or did she perhaps
Just perhaps
Have a spirit so free
She could wear a silver halo
And love wearing it
To Safeway?

THE SACRED IN US

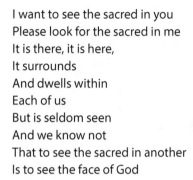

I want to see the sacred in you
Please look for the sacred in me
It is there, it is here,
It surrounds
And dwells within
Each of us
But is seldom seen
And we know not
That to see the sacred in another
Is to see the face of God

A GOOD MAN TO KEEP

I bought me a fancy red heart
With ribbons and lace all around
I bought it to send to my sweetheart
But then to my sorrow I found
My sweetheart had done run away
With a little blond dancer from Denver
If I could just find out her name
Believe me I know what I'd send her!

Well, so I hitched up my girdle
And then with my head held up high
I sent out that fancy red heart
Airmail! To some other guy!
Who knows now what's gonna happen
This could be a blessing disguised
I might meet Brad Pitt or a Redford
I'd never have found otherwise

And now the sky is the limit
I'm into a ball game that's new
This morning I truly had struck out
But now a home run could come true
That sweetheart who found the blond dancer
Can go take a high-flying leap
Cause I'm off now to follow my rainbow
And find a good man I can keep

A WOMAN OF GOOD

I heard it said of a woman of good,
"There are no shadows about her"
And I thought with wonder on those words
On a state so far from the known
No shadows of fear in the heart
No shadows of shame in the soul
No shadows of hate in the bone
No shadows of guilt in the mind.

To rejoice fully in the light
No shadows to block the warmth from the sun
To sleep dreamless sleep through the night
No ghostly shadows masking the moon
To give love and receive it with ease
No false shadows to tarnish the gift
Only the few become people of good
But life without shadows was the intent for us all

ACID ANGER

The acid bite of anger rose up in me
Stealing the good from my day
Just as flames stretching tall
Deprive air of its oxygen
Anger not for sins against self
But against one I hold dear
And not at one who was loathsome
But at one I had liked and respected
The anger etched itself in my mind
Yet left me nowhere to turn
For what happens with respect
When betrayal is witnessed

BELIEVE

Can you think how it must have felt?
She was young, virginal, so young
Perhaps working about her house
Perhaps seated at her loom
When suddenly, she was no longer alone
For standing there, before her eyes
Was an angel, an angel sent from God

Times were different then
Even so, angels were seldom seen
Mary must have wondered
Must have been frightened, confused
The angel told her not to have fear
That she was favored of God
That she would bear a Holy Child

And over her fear and confusion
Mary believed!
She knew that with God
All things were possible
Can you think that you would have believed?
Can you believe even now?
With God, all things are possible

BRANDING

Must man inflict pain?
Would a gentle nudge
Push the steer on through,
Or does it need the yell that produces fear,
And the goad that causes pain?
Must flesh be torn,
Or could the tag come out
By simply being unclipped?
We deplore the holocaust,
And rightfully so,
Yet I know those who deny its existence.
And, of course, never see
The tiny holocausts of each hour
Through which we live,
And die
And cause.

WHAT GOOD IS HE?

He was young and virile
Strong mind, strong muscle, strong cock
He loved the woman he married
And the children he fathered
Worked long hours to grow them
Hard, blue-collar job
Now his wife is dead
Children who knows where?
He is a ninety-year-old shell
Withered mind, withered muscle, withered cock
He cannot remember what he used to be
Except in small moments
Of consciousness
What good is that to him?
What good is he?

WOMAN IN THE PICTURE

She stands withered and still
Naked and alone
A figure lifeless with age
Her breasts are dry and empty
The dugs misshapen
The belly grown large
Under stretched and crumpled skin
Her eyes are hooded and dull
Without passion or sheen
And yet, a closer look
Reveals a depth that holds
Serenity and calm
There lies acceptance
For with the passing of youth
Comes a beauty of its own
Beauty based on sureness
That the fountains of her breasts
Nurtured life that yet lives on
That the warmth of her woman's womb
Grew within its dark folds
New souls that mirrored God
Spent passions and lost dreams
Pale beside this knowledge
I am humble at her feet
Her beauty is within
Her beauty is forever

EASTER COMES SOON

The sun gives no warmth and frost sears the land
The cold burns deep in the heart of man
But, snows will soon fade for winter does pass
And spring will bring joy to men's hearts at last
Yet ere that great day arrives for us all
The cruelest blow of the ages must fall
The one lonely Man of old Nazareth
Must take up His cross and walk to His death
He came to bring love, to save us He came
We turned Him away, now we bear the shame
We hung Him on high, we gave Him a crown
Then we pierced His side and, last, cut Him down
The grave, like the earth, then death did contain
No flowers, no life, just coldness and pain
But the grave, like the earth, became next a womb
And sent forth new life from out of the tomb
The stone rolled away and Christ lived anew
And man saw once more the rose touched with dew
Now Easter comes soon, as it does every year
Erasing the shame, the coldness, the fear
As true as the rainbow, God's covenant of rain
Does Easter proclaim that Christ lives again
The sun will give warmth, the roses will bloom
And our hearts can sing for Easter comes soon

ENDING

Life can leave in so many ways
It can take the unsuspecting in sleep
Or be a noisy eruption
Of discordant colors and sounds of war
It can inch out over time
Like the slow drip of a faucet
Painful breath after painful breath
With the clock of life
Slowing beyond understanding
And accidents that humiliate
And moans that cannot be held back

It can end in the arms of family
With love so very present
That it eases some pain
And dampens humiliation
Or it can end with only strangers
To change sheets and pretend care

She was my beloved friend
Much of life we had shared
I would wish her ending
To be peaceful and calm
I would wish her not to endure
The ticking of that clock
Or the pain of those difficult breaths
I would wish her surrounded by love
That she would feel deep in her soul

The truth is I am powerless
To change how her life will end
To grant her what I would wish
My only option being
To ask God to grant that
Her ending be peaceful and fast.

CAUSATION

We enslaved them years ago
When freed, we enslaved them again:
At the back of the bus
In poor schools
In ghetto housing
In low paying jobs
In laws that were unfair
In carefully constructed
Mythology which said:
They were less than we were
They were not smart
They shouldn't vote
They couldn't eat where we did
Couldn't drink the same water
That crossed our thin lips
One at a time they
Turned to drugs
United to become gangs
Used guns and fists
Stole from innocent folks
Seems like we made our own beds
Seems like we made theirs too

BURIED CHILD

She is buried
The child
How long?
Unknown
She was small
Her yearning
Simple
Mama's lap
Daddy's anger
Someone's touch

No touch felt
From friend or other
None truly expected
Lesson learned
To exist
Burial was required

Moldering
A form of life
Burial
A form of caress
No lap
No anger
But finally touch

GOD OF MY EXPERIENCE

The God of my experience
Indefinable, inexplicable
Essence rather than being
All encompassing "It"
Not bound by "He" or "She"
No image in my mind
Yet real beyond real
Randomness unthinkable
"Presence" alive in my soul
In every cell of my body
Every atom of the universe
Though I cannot understand
Yet I cannot deny

THE COWPOKE

While shepherds watched their flocks by night
All seated on the ground,
The angel of the Lord came down
And glory shone around, and glory shone around.
Now an old cowpoke was settin' on the hillside
He stared at all that glory, then he stood up and spoke,
"Now just a dern minute, Ma'am", he called.
The angel stopped in flight and looked back at him.
"You shouldn't oughta have done that", he said,
"This here is cattle country, Ma'am
And we don't cotton to them wooly sheep,
Ner to the shepherds that take care of 'em nuther,
And we sure don't take kindly to glory shinin' round 'em,
No offense of course, " as he tipped his hat.
"None taken," answered the angel dryly,
"But, fear not, my son,"
"For unto you is born this day
The baby Jesus who has love for all"
"I don't have no baby", said the cowpoke
"I don't even know where one is".
The angel smiled and answered,
"He is lying in a manger where cattle feed,
Where the ox and ass lie down together,
Where even the wooly sheep looks on in awe,
Where scripture says the shepherds came.
Now I'll admit it doesn't actually mention cowpokes
But likely they were somewhere about also."
"What happened there?" asked the cowpoke
"Well, the baby's mother smiled at those who came
While the baby Jesus gazed kindly on all.
So perhaps, my son, you could look kindly on shepherds
As Jesus looks kindly on you."

Red faced, the cowpoke took off his hat.
"Well, sure as tarnation I'll give it a try, Ma'am.
I reckon if He wants me to I'll give it a good try."
Then, with a mighty sweep of her great wings
The angel took to the heavens, saying as she went,
"That's all I can ask and He will help you succeed."
The bowlegged cowpoke pulled on his hat
Climbed on his horse and rode down the hill
Singing, as he rode, a lullaby to the sheep.

OLD TIMES TWO

They walked out the door
No word nor glance exchanged
Yet comfort could be felt
Ease with the known
No questions voiced
Answers past found
Is it to be envied?
This settled estate?
I do not know
Likely will never know
But I do not mourn
There is good in my freedom
So much to love
So much to learn
The universe is mine
Comfort is not all

FODDER

The sweat of mules
Mingled with that of soldiers
As they swore and strained
To push the great iron beast
Through the muddy trough
And up the rocky hill
At last in place it sat
Ugly and squat
Waiting to be fed
With the flesh of young men
Those who became
The fodder of war
Their only purpose
To slake the hunger
Of the manmade beast

IT ENDED

Life can end in a cataclysm
Exploding with violent colors
Or it can seep out slowly
With pain and soiled linens
A clock ticking slower and slower
Each breath pulled from resisting air
Finally refused by receiving tissue
However, it comes
It should not be alone
There should be love in the room
A hand to gently touch
I wished this for her
My wish was in vain

LONELY MAN

He walked among the crowd
And was unseen
He extended his hand
And was passed by
He uttered a pleading cry
And was not heard
The soul of lonely man

Darkness filled his eyes
For long and lonely years
When he could not see
That of the multitudes
who passed him by
Each man could claim to be
The soul of lonely man

Awareness slowly came
At last one day he knew
That someone must be first
To see and touch and hear
The task was his, not theirs
To reach and come to know
The soul of lonely man

THE CATAFALQUE

The catafalque rests
And on it the dream
A whisper
Meant to become
A song
A whisper
That became
A roar
Against nothing
Against nothingness
A whisper
Silenced
The catafalque rests
And on it the dream

STAR LIGHT

You have surely seen sunlight
When the sun rises on a cold winter day
It sets the icy branches aglitter
And melting snow from the rooftops
Cascades in rhythm to the ground
Each drop containing a rainbow
Placed there by the sunlight

You have surely seen moonlight
When the moon rises on a cold winter night
It dances between the dark clouds
And shines on snow covered ground
Weaving a carpet of diamonds
That crunch beneath every footfall
Diamonds placed there by the moonlight

You have surely seen starlight
As stars wink on in the dark winter sky
But have you seen starlight at the stable?
Where it turns the straw into gold
And softly shines on the babe
Who sleeps as the cattle stand watch
And the mother smiles on her child

ROOFING

They traverse the roofs with ease
Much as you would a paved road
Up one steep side and down another
Showing no fear nor seeming to falter
Often carrying heavy loads
They spring from one slope to another
As though born of mountain goats
Those loads they had brought up the ladders
Trip after trip after trip
Now they bend to pull up old shingles
They stoop to nail on the new
They rip off gutters with sharp edges
And carry tall stacks of torn tar paper
Atop their heads to the dumpster
Hour after wearying hour they do this
For days that start very early
And go for twelve hours at least
Oh, how their backs must ache
There are so many long buildings
That must seem to stretch to the horizon
They learn to live with exhaustion
Their skins are darker than mine
Not much English is heard
When I walk up to get the mail
Many avert their eyes
And don't answer if I speak
As though their skins were darker yet
And they had worked in the old deep south

Had been told don't look at the white lady
The job is honest labor but a hard way to live
Yet this feeds their children as we all must do
There is such ease in my life
I hope I can think to be grateful

TELLING TIME

Twice a week they came
And walked in the pool
The woman and the girl
The woman patient and serene
The girl in her twenties or more
And what? Slow? Challenged?
Developmentally Disabled?
I only know
If there is such a state as "Normal"
She had not reached that state
Or, perhaps was beyond it
She wanted to read the pool-side clock
She wanted to tell time
The mother would look at the girl
And explain the relationship of big and little hands
"When the big hand is on the twelve
And the little hand is on the two
That means it is two o'clock"
Do you remember your mother telling you that?
You heard it, you saw it and you learned it
The girl heard it, she saw it, but did not learn it
Over and over, day after day
She would ask
"Why is the big hand on the nine?
Why is the little hand between two numbers?"
Over and over, day after day
The mother would answer
With infinite patience, the same words
She had said many times before
Every time they came
The questions repeated themselves
Like the mindless ticking of that clock

Your mother knew you would learn
Her patience would surely pay off
The woman knew the girl would not learn
Yet she never grew sharp with the girl
She loved enough to be willing
To endure
What must have cut her heart deeply
Endless questions from the child she had borne
Who would never be what the mother had dreamed
For whom a new dream had to be found.

SNOW

And he shall purify
An age it seemed
The world stained
Lives soiled
Blighted by bitterness,
Sorrow,
Pain
Love eased
Yet vision still
Centered on stain
This night he sent
The purifying flakes
Virginal,
White
Delicate tracery
Cleansing my world
The faces glow
Awaiting the dawn
To be renewed
Yet,
Again
And he has purified

ABOUT THE AUTHOR

Rocky Rhoads has always had a love affair with words and a passion to put onto paper those that swirl around in her head. She has been able to do more of this since she retired as an RN at age 76 and moved from Arizona to Colorado. Now 85 years old she continues to reside in Colorado which she considers the land of her dreams. She enjoys a very active life.